Perfect World

I WAS SOOOO
Embarrassed!

by DEIRDRE BLIGH

Illustrated by
ANGELA MARTINI

SCHOLASTIC INC.

New York   Toronto   London   Auckland   Sydney

Mexico City   New Delhi   Hong Kong   Buenos Aires

FOR MY PARENTS, PHILIP AND DONNA, MY SISTER, ERIN,
AND MY HUSBAND, MARK BRIAN BLIGH—WHO HAVE WITNESSED
MANY OF MY EMBARRASSING MOMENTS, AND DECIDED
TO STICK WITH ME ANYWAY.

ISBN 0-439-80069-2

12 11 10 9 8 7 6 5 4 3 2 1   5 6 7 8 9 10/0

Printed in the U.S.A.
First printing, October 2005

Blushing.
That's the first sign.

The blushing is then accompanied by a slight change in body temperature, causing an even darker pink color in the cheeks. Your palms start to feel moist. The hair on your head starts to curl on its own (yes, even straight hair). You notice your clothes sticking to your body. The idea of being stranded on a desert island is suddenly appealing. And then it hits you—you are totally, completely, absolutely, one-hundred percent Embarrassed.

The good news is that pink is IN this season. So no matter how embarrassed you might look, you could still be in style. The bad news? This is not the last time you'll feel this way! Unfortunately, being embarrassed, humiliated, and downright horrified is a normal part of growing up. There is bound to be a step you are going to miss, a ridiculously funny costume you're going to get caught in, and a crush that's going to witness you doing the funky chicken.

Learn to laugh when you find yourself in these situations. Because if you can't laugh at yourself, it makes it a lot harder to handle some of the more difficult things in life.

If there's any consolation for embarrassing moments, it's that everyone has them! So grab a friend, or five, and race ahead (*not too fast now, I don't want you to trip and embarrass yourself*) to read about other girls' most shameful stories. And please feel free to laugh, chuckle—oh, just snort! I promise it'll make you feel good!

Education of Embarrassment

There are different degrees of discomfort. One person's minor slipup can be another person's excuse for finding life on Mars. Since you're a pro at taking quizzes, what better way to test your smarts in this sore subject? Think of some of your most recent or most memorable embarrassing moments, then answer the questions below. (Circle the answer that best fits):

1. When the incident occurred, my face felt like:
   a. lukewarm water
   b. hot chocolate
   c. burnt marshmallows

2. After my fall, it took me this long to get up:
   a. 30 seconds
   b. 2 minutes
   c. I'm still down for the count . . . can someone please help me up?!

3. When I collided with someone in the hall, I experienced:
   a. confusion
   b. dizziness
   c. a bruised ego

4. Afterwards, I felt:

    (a.) slightly less than larger than life

    b. pint-sized

    c. munchkins are cute, right?

5. It took people this long to stop talking about it:

    a. 1 afternoon

    (b.) 2 days

    c. they're still talking!

6. After reviewing the evidence, I would like to move to:

    a. the next town

    (b.) the next state

    c. the next galaxy

THE GRADES ARE IN

Now give yourself 1 point for every A,
2 points for every B, and 3 points for every C.

6-8: Fashionably Flustered

Relax! So you had a little mishap. Chances
are no one really noticed and you'll forget
about it just as quickly as it happened. And
your shirt is not even untucked. You truly
have it together, girlfriend. You are a role
model for humiliated girls everywhere.

9-11: Utterly Uncomfortable

Oh, you can handle this. I won't say
you don't have a reason to worry, but
soon you'll quickly get over this and
find the humor in it. Just as soon as
you get up off the floor and wipe that
mysterious substance off your
shirt . . .

12-14: Exclusively Embarrassed

Don't do it! I repeat, DO NOT let yourself cry! I'm sure everyone is laughing with you, not at you. But yes, this definitely entitles you to solitary confinement for the next 24 hours. Well, you can start with that.

15-18: Trend-Setting Traumatization

Okay, panic. Just give in to the feeling and freak out. You've really outdone yourself this time. Eventually, you and the entire school will get over it, but I'm not going to lie, it might take a while. Have you thought about homeschooling?

The Science of Making a Fool of Yourself

I hope you have a lab coat. And you better put on your safety goggles, too. Because the stories you are about to read are MESSY and GROSS!! These stories are so totally distressing, that you can't help but wonder if there was a science behind making them up!

GOT MILK?

Lunch is by far my favorite period. I get to sit with all my friends in the cafeteria and we just laugh the whole time! One afternoon, my friend was telling the funniest story I'd ever heard. I laughed so hard, that I lost all control of my bodily functions, and spit out all the milk that was in my mouth! Good thing, it only hit my friend across the table, and she wasn't too upset. Now mine is the funniest story told in school!

—Elisha

SINISTER SIBLING

YOU RATE IT! __1__

It was April Fool's Day, and I was feeling pretty lucky, because I hadn't had any jokes played on me. I got home from school and was thinking it would be pretty hilarious to pull a prank on my younger sister. She was usually the one tricking me, so it would be nice to get her back. I decided to use the powder room while planning my mischief. I wasn't even paying attention to what I was doing when I realized the joke was on me!

My devilish sister had placed Saran Wrap over the toilet seat! There's always next year.

—Erin

HE SAYS:

"NOBODY LOVES TO PLAY PRACTICAL JOKES MORE THAN GUYS. YOU GET A '10' IN MY BOOK FOR EVEN TRYING!"

P-U PIZZA

I always bring a lunch that my mom packs for me. But one Monday the cafeteria was having pizza, and I had a little bit of babysitting money, so I decided to splurge and buy myself some. Pizza is my favorite food, so it was a very special treat. Without thinking, I tossed my lunch on the top shelf of my locker, and planned on bringing it home that afternoon. On Friday, all the kids who had lockers near me were complaining about an awful smell. Then I remembered that it was my lunch from *Monday*! I was so embarrassed, that I stayed late after school to clean it up so no one would know it was mine!

—Sharone

HIP HINT

Owning a planner is a fabulous way to stay organized. You'll know when that English paper is due, which day you have soccer practice—and when the cafeteria is serving pizza!

MANLY MISHAP
P.E. PRANK

It was my first day at a new school, and I won't lie, I was pretty nervous. I had heard stories from my other friends about the tricks that the older guys liked to play, like stealing your clothes while you were in the gym shower. But my morning had gone smoothly, so I was feeling confident. That afternoon in my gym class, the teacher had us run a mile around the track. After all the sweating I did, I couldn't take a shower fast enough. As soon as I got back to my locker, I realized I had spoken too soon. All my clothes were missing, and I was forced to wear my sweaty, smelly gym clothes the rest of the day. And the stench was very noticeable. Good thing I had a whole year to redeem myself.

—Matt

THE HIGHS AND LOWS OF . . .

YOU RATE IT __4__

I was walking down the hallway with my BFF, and we were about to pass my crush going the opposite way. I decided to give him a high five but he didn't see me. Instead, I slapped him in the face, and gave him a bloody nose! After we cleaned up all the blood (with the exception of my crush who was sent to the nurse's office), I vowed to keep things on the down low from now on.

—*Jennifer*

FIELD TRIP FOLLIES

My class had planned a weekend field trip in the wilderness. Just my idea of fun—not! On the second day, we were scheduled to go on a nature walk in the woods. Just as I was thinking this was semi-cool, I was sprayed by a skunk! I tried to wash the smell off with multiple showers, but it just wouldn't go away! For the rest of the weekend, I smelled so bad, nobody wanted to get near me. But I couldn't blame them. I stunk so bad, I couldn't stand myself!

—*Abby*

TOP TEN EXCUSES FOR A BLUNDER

The trick to recovering from embarrassing situations is to . . . well, know the tricks to recovering from embarrassing situations! Here are some survival tips I've picked up along the way.

1. Change the subject

2. "Oh, I meant to do that."

3. Blame it on the floor (or the chair, door . . .)

4. Practicing for *America's Funniest Home Videos*

5. Didn't you know I was kidding?!?!

6. Lack of beauty sleep

7. Not eating your Wheaties

8. Forgetting to put in your contacts

9. Um . . . they must have just waxed the floors.

10. Untied shoelaces

STICKY SITUATION

Even though we weren't supposed to, I had been chewing gum in my biology class for the entire period. I was even bold enough to blow a few bubbles here and there when the teacher wasn't looking. Just before the period ended, I blew a huge bubble, and it popped all right—all over my hair! Of course after the loud noise I made, the teacher caught me, and sentenced me to detention for that afternoon.

But that's not even the worst part. The gum got stuck in my hair so badly, that I had to cut some of my hair to get it out! Nothing is worth losing your locks over!

—Amanda

HIP HINT

It's probably a wise idea to keep an emergency kit in your backpack—tissues, a needle and thread, and Band-Aids. Just in case you accidentally give your crush a bloody nose or something . . .

POTTY-TRAINED

I'm a neat freak. So when I arrive in the cafeteria for lunch, I usually inspect all the free seats before choosing one. But one afternoon, I was running late, and there was only one seat left at my friend's table, so I just sat down without thinking, *and* without inspecting it. As soon as my bottom hit the seat, I felt a cold, wet sensation on my pants. And let's just say that this was not an area of your pastel pants that you would ever want to be wet. I tried to dab the area dry, but for the rest of the afternoon, you couldn't deny that it looked like I had peed my pants! Everyone pointing and laughing at me didn't help my case, either.

—Lauren

MANLY MISHAP
EAU D' YUCK

I was getting ready to go to the Winter Wonderland dance, and I really wanted to make an impression on this girl that I liked. I thought if I wore a little cologne, it would make me a) smell good, and b) seem more mature than the other guys. I had never worn cologne before, so I snuck into my older brother's room, and just started spritzing—a little on the front of my neck, the back of my neck, behind my ears, on my left wrist, my right wrist, and one final dash, or four, on my shirt. I was feeling awfully handsome. When I got to the dance, I spotted my crush and mustered up the courage to walk over and say hello. Right after I said hi, she started sniffing the air and complaining of an awful smell. And then it hit me. "It's you!" she finally shouted. Apparently, there's such a thing as *too much* cologne. It was not the kind of attention I was hoping for that night.

—Mike

GROTESTQUE GREENS

YOU RATE IT _____

For breakfast, I normally eat on the run. One morning, my mom decided to make a home-cooked spread, including my favorite—spinach omelettes! I know it may sound disgusting, but it's really tasty. I quickly ate and headed off to school. That night, I happened to glance in the mirror, and something caused me to do a double-take—what was that ugly, green thing stuck in my teeth? Oh, just a chunk of spinach from my omelette that I had eaten seven hours ago! I couldn't believe that I went the entire day with food in my teeth, and nobody said anything! Maybe that explained why no one was making eye contact with me . . .

—Michele

HIP HINT

Brushing your teeth and flossing should totally be a part of your daily beauty regimen. Then you will always want to flash those pearly whites. (Notice it says "whites," and not "greens"??)

EXCUSE ME!

YOU RATE IT _____

I was sitting in study hall one afternoon and was feeling especially full. The cafeteria was serving Sloppy Joes that day, and they just weren't sitting well with me. All I needed was one good belch and I would feel soo much better! I was reading my book, when out of the blue, I let out the biggest burp! It happened so fast, I didn't even have time to try and hold it in like a true lady. Everybody started cracking up, and the guy in front of me turned around and said, "Mmm. Smells like Sloppy Joes to me!" So much for my manners!

—Aesha

HE SAYS: "BURPING IS THE BEST! NOW IF YOU COULD ONLY BELCH THE ALPHABET . . . "

Gym Clash

I advise you to stock up on
some Band-Aids, because I'm
afraid these stories are gonna
leave a mark! Gym never
seems to be the favorite class
of the day—unstylish
uniforms, smelly locker
rooms, the fear of getting
hit by a flying object. But it
seems the gymnasium is
not the only place where
physical bloopers occur.

HAZARDOUS HAMMOCK

My friend had invited me to her huge, family barbecue. I couldn't wait for some hot dogs and hamburgers "fresh off the barbi." My mouth was watering just thinking about it! I had fixed my plate with a little of everything and just needed a place to sit. But the only seat left was on the hammock. It would be a little difficult, but I was too excited to eat so I would have to manage. I was sitting with my plate on my lap for maybe a minute, before the hammock flipped onto the ground—and I landed facedown in my food! I knew I was hungry, but I would have preferred using a fork to eat!

—Denise

HIP HINT

Every young lady should demonstrate proper table manners in public. But they usually work best when used at a table. . . .

SCORE! (OR NOT)

My lacrosse team was having an awesome season. Our next game was against a team that
wasn't so good, so it should've been cake. But it
was a close game, and there wasn't much time
left on the clock. I finally got hold of the ball and
I ran like the wind toward the other end of the
field. I reached the goal, threw the ball in, and
started jumping up and down with joy. But why
wasn't anybody else on my team celebrating?
We just scored a goal, right? Turns out I was so
excited when I got the ball that I didn't notice I
was running toward the OTHER team's goal. No
wonder the goalie wasn't trying to stop me! I then
ran like the wind . . . straight home!

—Robin

ILL-FATED FASHIONISTA

My school was putting on a fall fashion show for charity, and I volunteered to be one of the runway models. Pumps were in that season, so they paired them with all of our different outfits. I wasn't used to wearing high-heeled shoes, so I was kind of hesitant. But I *was* a slave to fashion! I was strutting down the runway, modeling my last outfit of the show, when I tripped on the bottom of my gown and went sliding down the catwalk on my stomach! What had started as an ultrafashionable fundraiser, had quickly turned into a belly-flop!

—Jordan

HIP HINT

Standing straight helps with good posture and balance. Just the kind of balance a girl needs to walk comfortably in heels!

EYE SHADOW

I was the catcher for my girls' softball team. I didn't mind playing that position because I got to wear a face mask, and always felt protected. But as you may know, the catcher is also required to hit the ball. It wasn't my favorite part of the game, but I tried my best. During one of our Saturday games, I must have been preoccupied with my dance performance that night, because I looked away for a minute, and just as I turned my head back around, WHAM! The ball made direct contact with my left eye! I was left with no home run and a nice shiner. Needless to say, I did not need to wear much eye makeup to bring out my eyes that night!

—Jasmine

HE SAYS: "BEING ABLE TO DANCE *AND* PLAY A SPORT IS AWESOME. GUYS DIG GIRLS WHO ARE MULTITALENTED."

DECORATION DISASTER

My school has this tradition of decorating a Christmas tree and lighting a menorah each year, and I was a member of the holiday committee. Part of the reason I volunteered (okay, the only reason), was because my flame-of-the-moment was also helping out. We paired off and started with the top of the tree. He was handing me the ornaments while I stood on a chair to hang them. I must have lost my balance, because before I could stop myself, I fell back off the chair and landed right on top of my crush! Thankfully, he wasn't hurt. But boy, did I feel silly. 'Tis the season for embarrassing moments! Guess I truly was "crushing" on him!

—Carrie

HOW HARD ARE YOU CRUSHING?

When you see him, your whole world turns upside down. The mere mention of his name gets your lazy bones out of bed most mornings! So you're allowed to lose your composure every once in a while. Diagnose just how badly you've been bitten by this love bug by answering the quiz below. Then follow the recommendations for recovery, and call your best friend in the morning!

(Circle the symptom that best fits):

1. When I pass my crush in the hall, I:
    a. smile.
    b. look away.
    c. freeze up and forget who I am!

2. I know this much information about my crush:
    a. name
    b. name and address
    c. if the FBI knew how much I *did* know, they would recruit me.

3. I talk to my crush:

   a. once in a while.

   b. every day.

   c. Talk? As in speak with words?

4. When I see my crush, my pulse:

   a. speeds up a little.

   b. races.

   c. Can you repeat the question? I couldn't hear you over my heartbeat.

5. My crush knows me:

   a. barely

   b. pretty well

   c. all too well, ever since I left my name on his "anonymous" Valentine card

6. My crush could best be described as:

   a. admiration

   b. infatuation

   c. I'd like to speak to my lawyer before answering.

Now give yourself 1 point for every A, 2 points for every B, and 3 points for every C.

6-8: SLIGHTLY SENTIMENTAL

How sweet, you have a little crush! You haven't gotten the courage to talk to him yet, but you're perfectly content with just staring at him every day. You should start getting his attention by making eye contact and smiling. Chances are he will also start looking at *you* in a different way!

9-11: RIDICULOUSLY ROMANTIC

You envision the day when he waltzes over to you in the middle of a crowded hallway and professes his undying love to you. The problem is you've only talked a few times, and he doesn't have a clue how you feel! Instead of chatting about school and homework, bring up some other sub-jects—like what he does on the weekends. If you are both interested in the same activities, you can suggest making some plans!

12-14: *ABSOLUTE ADORATION*

You're bummin'. You're friends with him and hang out all the time, but he still doesn't get that you like him—like *really* like him. Maybe it's time to use your body language to let him know that you're into him as more than a friend. Try sitting a little closer to him at the movies, or grabbing his hand while you're walking in the mall. He won't need Morse code for those signs!

15-18: *TOTALLY TRIPPIN'*

You're about to explode! You've done the eye contact thing, the hanging out thing, *and* the body language thing. And the boy is totally in the dark. It's time to . . . get ready . . . you can do this! Tell him how you feel! Maybe he is just too nervous to bring up the topic first. But this is one subject you don't want to fail!

FALL FROM GRACE

I was really big into ballet—I took classes every day and had just graduated to dancing *en pointe*, or on my toes. My friends were always trying to get me to show off some of my moves, but I would always get shy and say no. One day during gym class, my friends started egging me on again about showing them some dance steps. I finally gave in. There was a stack of floor mats nearby, and I was going to attempt to do a *grand jeté*, or giant leap, over them. I leaped right over the mats, and landed on my rear on the hard, linoleum floor. Not only was my pride hurt, but my *derrière* was killing me! I ended up breaking my tailbone and having to use a special pillow every time I sat down for the rest of the year! I knew being humble had its advantages.

—Dori

HIP HINT

It's great to be involved in different activities with your school. They can help you decide what you want to be when you grow up . . . interior decorator, anyone?!

MANLY MISHAP

KEEP YOUR EYE ON THE BALL

YOU RATE IT _____

I was totally into this girl in my grade. I mean, she was gorgeous! I had soccer practice on the field right next to the track, where she ran with the track team. I must have been a little too focused on her, because just as she was passing, one of the guys on my team came up behind me and pulled my shorts down! There I was, standing with my shorts around my ankles, while the most beautiful girl stared at my underwear! This was definitely not going to help me overcome my shyness!

—Mark

SOAP OPERA

YOU RATE IT _____

After cheerleading practice, I decided to take a shower before I went home. The girls' locker room was practically empty, so I thought I could get away with belting out some show tunes. The next morning, I was sitting in my homeroom when I heard something all too familiar over the PA system. It was my VOICE! Someone must have thought it would be hilarious to record me singing in the shower and play it for the entire middle school to hear! Well, that person wasn't the only one who found it so funny. . . .

—Jackie

SPEEDY GONZALEZ

I had just gotten some new Rollerblades for my birthday, and I was dying to try them out. I buckled myself in, and started on my way. I was pretty successful on my rather flat street, so I thought I'd challenge myself on a hill. All of a sudden, I was flying down this street! The only way I could stop myself was to swerve and crash into someone's bushes! Flat land was looking really good about then.

—Kelly

HIP HINT
Challenging yourself can help you overcome your fears. But no one said you couldn't challenge yourself on flat terrain!

SKI BUNNY

I went skiing for the very first time with my friend and her dad. We had just gotten on the ski lift, ready to descend our first slope of the day. I was sitting by myself, taking in the beautiful snowcapped mountains. I was getting closer to the top, and I just assumed the ski lift would stop and let me off. Nope! The ski lift kept on going down the mountain! My friend and her dad were yelling at me to get off, but I didn't know how! Everyone behind me was laughing at me on my way back down. Good thing I enjoyed the view.

—Rachel

SHE SHOOTS, SHE SMELLS!

My P.E. class was in the middle of a basketball game. All that running around was causing me to break into a sweat. The more I sweat, the more I kept smelling a foul odor. I had put deodorant on, so it wasn't that—it was garlic! I had a very garlic-y meal the night before, and it was oozing out of my pores! Toward the end of the game, everyone had caught wind— literally—of my scent.

—Domenica

"Social Studies"

Sure, you're supposed to be studying up on your history, grammar, and math. But isn't it more fun to be studying the cutie in your class or the new fashion must-haves for the season? Good answer!

"JUST BROWSING"

YOU RATE IT _____

My friends and I always looked forward to hanging out at lunch, despite the fact that every day this one upperclassman came over and picked on us. Well, one day I decided I had enough. It was time for me to break out of my shell and stick up for my friends! It's called girl power, right? Wrong. It's called complete humiliation. Right after I told him to "try picking on someone his own size," he looked at me, while the entire cafeteria listened, and said, "Why don't you do something about that unibrow!" The unibrow has since disappeared. And I don't think anybody is missing it. . . .

—Whitney

HE SAYS: "IT'S MAJORLY COOL HOW YOU STICK UP FOR YOUR FRIENDS. RIGHT ON."

JUNK-FOOD JUNKIE

One Friday night, my friend invited a bunch of us to her house for a sleepover. I loved sleepovers! We watched the newest Orlando Bloom movie, talked about our latest crushes, and my favorite—ate lots and lots of junk food! My girlfriends and I were sitting around swapping room-decorating tips, when I started feeling really nauseous. I waited for a couple of minutes, hoping that the feeling would subside, but it was too late. I turned to my right and threw up all over my friend's lap! Looks like I'll be staying away from sugar for a while.

—*Meghan*

HIP HINT

When going away for a week, a weekend, or just a night, it's always smart to pack an extra outfit—or pajamas. You never know . . . one of these sleepovers it might be **your** lap!

CALL THE FASHION POLICE!

Forgetful is my middle name. So it was no surprise when I forgot to bring home one of my books for a homework assignment due the next day. *No big deal*, I thought, *I'll just go in early and finish it*. Because it was winter, it was still dark out the next morning when I got up. And I was so out of it, I didn't even bother turning on the light when I got dressed. When I finally had a minute to breathe at the end of the morning, I looked down at my outfit. I had committed the ultimate fashion *faux pas*! What I thought was an acceptable and chic gray sweater, was actually the hideous Christmas gift from my grandma this year—a gray sweater with a reindeer on the front!

—*Nicki*

HIP HINT

Never shy away from standing out. Some of the greatest fashion designers got their big breaks just by being a little different! (Although, it's probably safe to assume that reindeer will never be "in"...)

TALK ABOUT AN ICEBREAKER

I had just moved to a new town and was eager to make friends. I was thrilled when this girl I just met asked me to come over for a party. We were all sitting around in a circle, playing Truth or Dare. It was my turn, and I chose Truth. I figured that was my safest bet since I didn't really know anybody. The question was whether or not I thought anybody in our class was cute, and if so, who it was. Well, that was easy! I described this one boy I had noticed, but didn't know his name. All the other girls started laughing uncontrollably as I sat there very confused. It turns out that my new dreamboat was this girl's brother! I knew I should've picked Dare!

—Sophia

HEAR YE, HEAR YE

YOU RATE IT! _____

We were studying Victorian literature in my English class, so my teacher assigned us to write a speech about a popular food from that period. She allowed us to use our outlines when we stood in front of the room (thank God!). I had just started on my last page, almost finished describing bread pudding, when I noticed everyone laughing. I immediately looked down, and I had started reading a love note that a boy in my class (that I do not like!) had passed to me the day before! I must have accidentally grabbed it out of my folder with my speech! After that, I wished I could have traveled back to the Victorian era . . . and stayed there!

—Tatiana

HIP HINT:

When speaking in public, make sure to talk slowly and clearly. When reading a love note from an unwanted admirer, talk very fast and muddle all words!

THE GREEN GOBLIN

YOU RATE IT _____

My parents had gone out for the evening, so I decided to treat myself to some girly pampering. I took a bubble bath, painted my nails, and thought I would try this new face mask. Of course, my dog had to go to the bathroom right in the middle of my spa session. It was doubtful I would run into anybody, so I took Fifi outside, mask and all. All of a sudden, Fifi heard another dog bark and took off! I started chasing after her, when I noticed the hottie from down the street, standing in front of his house. I tried to wave and smile, but he was just staring at me with this frightened look on his face. Then I remembered that I had that fluorescent green mask on my face! Yeah, I finally caught Fifi, but is that really the most important part of this story?! Hottie, people, HOTTIE!

—Caroline

TOP TEN REASONS WHY IT'S IMPORTANT TO LAUGH AT YOURSELF

You don't need to visit
a fortune-teller to know there are
miserable moments that lie ahead. However,
you won't be able to predict *when* they're
going to happen. So the key is knowing
beforehand how to laugh them off.
Then you can be perfectly prepared
in the event of a blunder!

1. If you're laughing, no one will think it's
   a big deal.

2. Laughing shows everyone you have a positive
   attitude (is there any other kind?!).

3. Sometimes forcing yourself to smile on the
   outside can make you feel happy on the inside.

4. Laughter acts as a stress-reducer, and there-
   fore stimulates creativity.

5. Giggling is contagious. What a great way to make friends!

6. Laughter gives the muscles in the chest, neck, abdomen, shoulder, face, and scalp a workout. Whew.

7. Laughter's been proven to boost information retention. You could use some of that, right?

8. Researchers say you will stay healthier if you laugh 15 to 20 times a day. Get started!

9. Guys love a girl who's confident enough to laugh at herself!

10. You don't need a reason! Just start . . . someone is bound to join in sooner or later!

MANLY MISHAP
FOREIGN FOUL-UP

Lucky for me, in my French class I got to sit next to the girl I had a crush on. One day during class, she dropped her pencil. I thought it would be a nice gesture if I picked it up for her. I bent over into the aisle, and my entire desk tipped over! I didn't manage to get her pencil, but I did get a nice round of applause from everyone in my class. As the French would say, *"C'est la vie!"* . . . I guess.

—*Philip*

WALK OF SHAME

I had my eye on the same boy for a couple of years. It just so happened that he lived on my street. One morning, while my younger brother and I were walking to school, he joined us. My brother looked at him, then turned to me and asked, "Isn't this the same boy that's postered all over your room?" My face turned from "peachy keen" to ruby red. Luckily, my crush was flattered and just smiled.

—*Jess*

SPF 0

It was the weekend before my class pictures, a
I swore to myself that this year I would not mes
mine up (the year before, I forgot
which day we were taking pictures,
and I was wearing the most out-of-date
shirt and not a stitch of lip gloss!).
It was still beach weather,
so I figured if I laid out that
Sunday, I would have a sun-
kissed glow for my picture. I have
darker skin, so I didn't put on any sun-
block so I could really get some color.
That was my first mistake. My second
mistake was falling asleep on the beach for two
hours while I cooked like a lobster! I was red from
head to toe. My face was so sunburned that everyone at school kept asking me if I was crying! Well,
there's always next year.

—Jane

HIP HINT

Always protect your skin from the sun!
Or be mistaken for a student posing as a
supersize tomato. The choice is yours.

AWKWARD ADOLESCENCE

I was waiting for my mom to pick me up after school. My crush walked over and asked to borrow some money for the pay phone. Umm, of course! I opened my backpack to get out some change, and a whole bunch of books fell out—the one he happened to pick up was for girls about their bodies changing! I could not believe he was looking at that! From that point on, I felt so self-conscious every time I passed him in the hall. I think that alone might have stunted my growth spurt that year!

—Daniella

HE SAYS: "GIRLS MAY NOT KNOW THIS, BUT GUYS GO THROUGH SOME CHANGES, TOO. SO, WE UNDERSTAND MORE THAN YOU THINK."

BLUSHING BRIDESMAID

YOU RATE IT _____

My older cousin was getting married, and she asked me to be her junior bridesmaid. Getting all dolled-up in some pink, froo-froo outfit was the last thing I wanted to do. But I didn't have much say in the matter. I was having a good time dancing at the reception, when I suddenly felt a cool breeze around my legs, which was weird since my dress was floor-length. Somebody must have stepped on the bottom of my dress while I was cutting a rug, because the whole bottom half had been ripped off! My entire family was now staring at my froo-froo underwear! And the bride thought she would be the center of attention that day!

—Gina

HAPLESS HAIRCUT

My bangs needed a trim—bad. Cutting hair didn't seem like brain surgery, so I decided to give it a whirl. I couldn't get them to look even, so I kept trimming . . . and trimming . . . and trimming some more . . . until they were really short, really uneven, and just plain hideous! How could I bear school the next day?! It  then made perfect sense to me why my hairstylist has one of those special certificates!

—Tracy

Extracurricular Embarrassment

Just because it didn't happen
in pre-algebra, or on school
premises, doesn't mean you
can't fail with flying colors.
Just when home ec became
your favorite class, or you
couldn't wait for the weekends, the "art" of uneasiness
had to rear its ugly head.

HEAD AND SHOULDERS

In my opinion, cooking was the best class of the week. Because—hello!—we get to bake delicious things and eat them! This particular week, we were baking snickerdoodles—ya know, the cinnamon sugar cookies? They're to die for! After we put our cookies in the oven, my group and I had to clean up our mess. I looked over at my friend, and noticed some white specks in her hair. I told her she must have gotten some flour in her hair, and started patting her head. Turns out that it was not flour at all, but some dandruff! How was I supposed to know? I apologized a hundred times, but I still felt terrible. I couldn't even enjoy my cookies after that.

—Lindsay

RAISE YOUR VOICE

I love to sing, but have a terrible voice. So I was psyched about my new chorus class, where I get to sing with other people and not be heard as much. We were asked to perform a couple of songs at the annual holiday assembly. I was so into it, singing at the top of my lungs with my eyes closed, that I didn't realize the song had ended and the entire auditorium was listening to my voice and my voice alone! How humiliating! So much for my singing career.

—Hayley

"WEB" OF LIES

YOU RATE IT _____

I was IM'ing with this boy Mark from my class. I knew he had a serious crush on me, but he had always been just a friend and nothing more. I left my room for a minute to get a snack, and my sister got on the computer. She told Mark I was madly in love with him and wanted to be his girl-friend! The next day he told everyone at school I had finally professed my love to him. It took a whole month to convince him—and my entire class—that it was my sister!

—Natasha

CULTURE SHOCK

I was so excited about my family's upcoming trip to England. I'd never been to Europe before. After lunch, I saw my cutie crush in the hall  and started to tell him about how my dad was going to get us tickets to a football game while we were there, and that I hoped we got to sit on the 50-yard line. My guy laughed a little and then informed me that English football is what Americans call soccer. How was I supposed to know? At least there will be cute boys in uniforms. . . .

—Liz

PUZZLING POLITICS

My school was holding class elections, and I decided to run for class president. I made pins, T-shirts, and posters. I also photocopied a bunch of flyers with my name and slogan on them, and posted them all over the school. One day, my best friend came up to me and said, "Funny, I always thought you spelled your name with an 'h'." I do! I had spelled my name wrong on every single poster I put up! Who was going to vote for a class president that couldn't even spell her own name?!

—Sarah

HOMEMADE HUMILIATION

Since you're having so much fun reading other people's most embarrassing moments, why not make up a few of your own? Take turns with your best friend, asking each other for the words in parenthesis. After she fills in your words, she will read back to you your very own mortifying moment, then you can do the same for her!

EMBARRASSING MOMENT #1:

"My best friend and I got backstage passes for

_____ concert. When I met the lead singer, I
(music group)

totally _____ on my _____,
       (verb ending in –ed)   (clothing item)

and landed right on the snack table. There were,

like _____ people staring at me! I was soo
      (a number)

_____. At least, I didn't _____."
     (adjective)   (verb)

EMBARRASSING MOMENT #2:

"There was this guy I was totally _____ about.

(adjective)

One day in _____ I ran up behind _____

(school subject)　　　　　　　　　(male friend's name)

and _____ his _____.

(verb ending in -ed)　　　　(article of clothing)

Only it wasn't him, it was my crush! The guy was

_____ and he had this _____

(verb ending in –ing)　　　　　　　(adjective)

look on his face. I was _____. I never

(adjective)

_____ at him again."

(verb ending in –ed)

EMBARRASSING MOMENT #3:

"I was in the middle of my _____ game
                                    (sport you play)

when my _____ got caught on a _____
            (body part)   (noun)

and I totally _____ and fell flat on my
                    (verb ending in –ed)

_____. I looked up and the entire _____
(body part)   (name of sports team)

was _____ at me. Man, was
            (verb ending in –ing)

I _____."
     (adjective)

EMBARRASSING MOMENT #4:

"I was walking up to the podium to give my election

speech, when I tripped on my _____!
(article of clothing)

I went sliding down the aisle on my _____,
(body part)

and landed right next to _____!
(one of crush's names)

I was _____! After that, every time
(adjective ending in -ed)

I see him in the hall, he starts _____
(verb ending in -ing)

at me!"

Remember to always proofread homework or projects before handing them in! If you ever spell your own name wrong by mistake—immediately disown all work, followed by putting in for school transfer.

DANCING QUEEN

There was a new, scary movie playing and I really wanted to go with my friends to see it. Only problem was that I was broke as a joke! So my mom said she would give me the money if I mopped the kitchen floor. Deal! It wasn't like I was going to run into cute boys or anything, so I stayed in my pajamas, put my headphones on, and embraced the mop. I must not have heard the doorbell ring, because there I was singing my heart out, when I noticed my mom and a boy from my class in the doorway hysterically laughing at me! I totally forgot he had mentioned coming over to borrow a book. The next week at school, he told everyone about my recital, and they started calling me the "Dancing Queen." Did I mention I was in my pajamas??

—Brandy

MANLY MISHAP
LIVING ART

Art is not my strong point. This explains why I was up till the wee hours of the morning the night before my final project was due. I was so tired, that I slept right through my alarm, barely making it to school on time. My art class was in the morning, and my teacher decided that we were going to present our projects to the whole class. My turn finally came, and I started talking about my drawing. Halfway through my presentation, everyone burst out laughing and started pointing at me—including the teacher! I may not be van Gogh, but I didn't think my project was that bad! Turns out that when I fell asleep on my masterpiece, all the ink from my drawing had gotten on my forehead. I always knew *I* was a work of art!

—Brett

AND THE AWARD GOES TO . . .

My dad thinks it's "memorable" to videotape my younger sister and I. One weekend, we decided to clean out the attic. We found a ton of boxes with my mom's old clothes, so we started trying them on and acting goofy. I have to admit, I was having a lot of fun. That Monday, everyone in my English class had to bring in a video of them giving a speech at home. My teacher started playing mine, and there I was, dressed in my mom's old bell-bottoms, hamming it up in front of the camera! I must have grabbed the wrong tape before I left the house! Not the break into show business I was looking for.

—Ali

HE SAYS: "BELIEVE IT OR NOT, GUYS LOVE ACTING SILLY. AND THEY'RE ALWAYS LOOKING FOR AN ACCOMPLICE."

FIESTA!

For my birthday, my family took me to my favorite Mexican restaurant for dinner. Everything was great until they brought out my dessert. One of my family members must have mentioned that it was my birthday, because before I had a chance to run and hide, the entire wait staff came out singing loudly and playing maracas! When they got to the table, they put a sombrero on my head and made ME play one of

the maracas! I was mortified. Little did I know
that one of the onlookers was a guy in my class.
He must have told everyone at school, because
people kept asking me why I wasn't in the band:
"Because we heard you play a mean maraca!"

—Kate

LINE, PLEASE!

YOU RATE IT _____

There was nothing more I hated than being
onstage. But my entire grade was required to
participate in a school play about the immigrants
who came to America. I was cast as Lady Liberty.
It was the perfect role for me, since I didn't have
to speak a lot. The big night arrived, and I was
so nervous! I just kept telling myself there was
nothing to worry about—I could handle two lines!
Well, the time came for my lines . . . and went.
My drama teacher had to eventually whisper the
lines to me from the wings. The whole audience
heard, and started laughing! The Statue of Liberty
would have done a better job.

—Melika

FAKING THE FLUTE

My parents really wanted me to play in the band.
I wasn't so into it, but I said okay to make them
happy. The flute seemed like it would be the easi-
est instrument to learn. But it ended up being
really, really hard! I didn't practice as much as I
was supposed to, so I always sounded like a dying
bird. We had a recital coming up, and I was totally
unprepared. The band was pretty big and loud
without me, so I just pretended to play the keys,
blowing air into my flute. I was unaware that there
was a part of one of the songs where the *small* flute
section plays by themselves. So when all the
other instruments stopped playing, I was sitting there making the most out-of-tune and
off-key noises! It sounded horrible. I
made my parents happy all right.
Happy to go home that night!

—Marie

MANLY MISHAP
BOMBS AWAY!

I'm petrified of heights. But it was summer, and I was not going to sit out another cannonball contest. I would just have to overcome my fear of the high dive. I finally got up the nerve and climbed the ladder. Then I went for it! But halfway down, I got scared! I landed facedown on my stomach. That was gonna leave a mark! When I got out of the water, everyone was asking me if I was okay. The stinging sensation on my stomach lasted for two days!

—Tim

MOVIE MAYHEM

About once a month, my parents like to plan a "family outing." This usually entails all of us participating in the same activity, and most often against our will. This particular time, it was decided we'd all go to a movie. That I could handle—no lights, no talking, done! So my mom, my dad, my sister, my brother, and I pile into the theater, take our seats, sit back, and relax. Halfway through the movie, my dad starts snoring—and I mean, the NOISY kind of snoring that you can't ignore! I finally nudged him and he woke up. If you're going to plan an outing, the least you can do is stay awake for it!!

—Stephanie

Congratulations!

You have OFFICIALLY completed your unofficial course in the art of over-coming *embarrassing moments!* You must be exhausted after all the chortling, chuckling, and cackling you've done. You've witnessed the not-so-good, the bad, and the *downright ugly.* But you must know that all the victims of these ridiculously funny stories (they were pretty funny, weren't they?!) are *a-okay.* They were able to pick themselves up, dust themselves off, and get on with their fabulous lives. Someone, somewhere along the way, must have also encour-aged them to *learn how to laugh* at themselves in these situations. And once they did that, they realized that the situation wasn't so bad afterall.

So my hope for you is to SLOWLY WALK away with some lasting thoughts.

Number one: Be proud of who you are, and how you have overcome all of life's obstacles thus far. You go, girl.

Number two: Welcome any road-blocks that lie ahead, because you are now fully equipped to handle them. With some serious style.

Number three, and perhaps most important: Never take things too seriously. Because if you never take things too seriously, you'll never get hurt. And if you never get hurt, you'll always have fun. And having fun is really the key to a successful life. Take it from a proclaimed expert in the field of embarrassment—how else did you think I could write this book?!